MASTER BUILDER

The Unofficial

Island Builders

Handbook

TRIUMPH
B O O K S

This book is available in quantity at special discounts for your group or organization.
For further information, contact:

Triumph Books LLC
814 North Franklin Street
Chicago, Illinois 60610
Phone: (312) 337-0747
www.triumphbooks.com

Printed in U.S.A.
ISBN: 978-1-62937-864-0

Interior design: Patricia Frey
Cover design: Jonathan Hahn

Contents

Phoebe

I was thinking about how to thank you, and I came up with a recipe for a leaf umbrella!

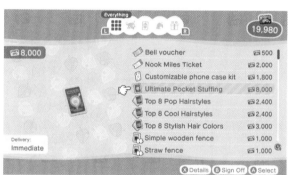 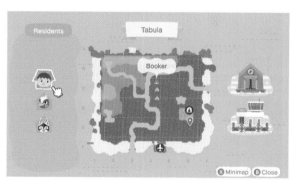

I caught a clown fish!
How many can fit in a carfish?

Introduction

It's difficult to point out exactly what makes the Animal Crossing series so wonderful. Perhaps it's because this gentle community simulator offers so many different things for players to dive into. Perhaps you enjoy building up a dream house, decorating each room according to a master plan of your own design. Or maybe your ambitions drive you to micromanage a town, laying out every building and honing every natural feature to perfection. Then again, maybe your home is just a place to put your excess fish as you work to harvest resources to build a financial empire.

Whatever your approach, this is probably the best time to be an Animal Crossing player. The latest entry has been a runaway success for Nintendo, which means

that it's easier than ever to find other people to share items, ideas, and even multiplayer sessions. In fact, the popularity of New Horizons even took Nintendo by surprise. The game sold nearly 12 million copies in the first two weeks it was available – more than the company expected it to sell throughout the game's total lifetime. Celebrities like Elijah Wood, Brie Larson, and Chrissy Teigen are among its fans, with some of those big names even dropping into strangers' towns for visits.

And let's face it – the timing couldn't have been better for a new Animal Crossing. Fans had already been eagerly awaiting New Horizons' release, since it had been more than a decade since a main entry in the series was available on a home console. When it finally hit the Nintendo Switch on March 20, 2020, much of the world was staying home as a response to the COVID-19 pandemic. The game's friendly vibe and relaxing gameplay gave many players a social outlet during a time where social

distancing was becoming the new normal. In New Horizons, players can visit with their friends, have sleepovers, and participate in outdoor activities – all from the comfort, and safety, of home.

Regardless of what drew you to the series, there aren't any wrong ways to approach Animal Crossing. Whether you've been playing since the GameCube days or this is your first interaction with Tom Nook and the crew, welcome. This book is designed to introduce you to many of the core activities and mechanics behind Animal Crossing: New Horizons. New players will find a solid introduction to many of the activities and underlying mechanics behind the game, designed to give you a head start in this relaxing world. Even experienced fans may find a few new tips or methods to propel their gameplay to the next level.

If you find yourself overwhelmed by the options and possibilities that New

Horizons offers, don't worry. We'll help you get your bearings and show you how to dial into the elements that you find the most enjoyable. While it's absolutely true that you can take New Horizons at your own pace, it definitely pays to be smart about it. We'll highlight some recommended steps that you can take so that you don't end up wasting time or energy. There aren't many lasting consequences to the Animal Crossing experience, and experimentation can be a rewarding facet of the game, but players who are looking for a little nudge in the right direction have come to the right place.

All right! Are you ready? Well, let's get to it then. Don't worry about packing your bag, since we'll be traveling light on this trip. Tom Nook is providing an all-inclusive getaway package, but be prepared to rough it for the first few days…

My new life is underway...
I can do whatever I want!
WOO-HOO!

Getting Started

Animal Crossing: New Horizons starts out differently from past games in the series. This time, you're not visiting an established town. Instead, you're part of its creation! You begin your journey on a new island as part of a getaway vacation package. Over the course of several weeks, you've got a lot to do. So much so, in fact, that it might be a little overwhelming at first. Take a deep breath. Relax! The point of Animal Crossing is to have a good time. You don't have to worry about losing lives or making a lot of decisions with lasting consequences.

Although there are a few exceptions, most of the choices you make can be revisited later on, once you have a better sense of the kind of Animal Crossing experience you're looking for. In the meantime, let's walk through some of the important aspects of the first few days of your journey.

Island Representative

Before you get started, there's one critically important thing about the game that you should know, particularly if you plan on sharing your island with other players in your household. Your Switch console can only support one island at a time – no matter how many copies of the cartridge you buy. Up to eight players can share that island, provided they each have an individual user account on the Switch. That's a fairly traditional approach for the series, but newer players may not expect that limitation. Four of those players can explore the island simultaneously via local co-op, but we'll get into that a little later.

The first person who starts playing the game will have special duties and responsibilities, as Tom Nook's designated Island Representative. If you're planning on playing New Horizons

> **Tom Nook**
> Yes, yes! I hereby name you the Resident Representative of Tabula!

Be sure the first player on your island is someone who's going to stick with it!

as a household, make sure that person is someone who's going to be an active player – especially in the early weeks of the game. For example, the Island Representative is the only player who can choose where shops and other buildings will be placed. They're also the player who can choose where ramps and bridges can go later on in the game, which are huge quality-of-life improvements for all players on that island. In addition to the responsibility of placing these structures, the Island Representative will be responsible for gathering materials and paying for much of it, too.

Part of the fun in New Horizons comes from watching the island steadily improve over time. That progress can be halted entirely if the Island Representative loses interest in the game or can't check in as regularly as other players may want. If you don't plan on sharing the game with other members of your household, you're in the clear. Otherwise, save yourself some potential headaches and make sure that your most passionate player is in the Island Representative role. You'll thank us later.

Picking Your Place

During the opening section of the game, Timmy and Tommy Nook walk you through the basics, such as your character's name and starting appearance. The name you choose sticks with you throughout the game, but don't feel locked into how your character looks in those early moments. You'll have plenty of additional options for swapping out hairstyles, clothing, and much more. One thing you may want to spend some

Don't like your choices?

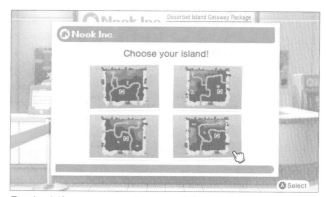

Restart the game and try again!

Once you commit, you're locked in.

You can't move the plaza location, which includes the island-services tent.

time considering, however, is the layout of your island.

The Nooks will present you with four possible islands. Don't feel bad if you don't know exactly what you're looking at. Every island will have a branching river, a pond or two, a pier, an airport, a northern beach, and a plaza. Additionally, islands will all contain three different elevations. The layouts of these various elements are randomized.

The plaza location is the big thing to look out for. It's the icon that looks like a leaf with a little bite taken out of it. That plaza will essentially be the heart of your island, and it's one of the few things (along with the pier, airport, and the northern beach) that you can't move

This tent houses many important functions. Don't worry, it'll get bigger.

later. You'll eventually gain the ability to fill in rivers, carve through cliffsides, and essentially shape the land to your specifications, but that won't come for a few weeks of real time. Because of that, it's a good idea to try to find a layout that has a nice long stretch of uninterrupted beach (for fishing) and a centrally located plaza.

If you don't see an island that you're interested in, you can close the game and restart it. You'll have to go through the character-creation portion again, but it's better to do that than to commit to a location that you're not excited about. Again, you'll be able to change things significantly later on, but all's not lost if you think the initial options are bummers.

to craft items in the new DIY system, and get to know some of the other starting villagers. There's a lot of info to soak in, and some of it isn't completely explained. Here are a few additional tips to help you get started in this new world.

Some Starting Odds and Ends

Once you've created your character and chosen an island, you're off! The next hour or so of the game covers the basics, broadly speaking. You'll place your tent, learn how to forage for basic materials and how to use those materials

■ Leave some walking space! The game will allow you to put your tent and other buildings close to the edge of rivers and ponds. If you plan on doing any fishing (and you are probably going to be doing some fishing), that placement isn't ideal. It's best to leave a space or two between the boundary of your buildings and those bodies of water, so you can walk past without having to walk around. If you goof up, you

Putting your tent this close to the water will make it annoying to walk around

Give it a little space, and that way you can fish without having to go out of your way.

can fix it later on once you unlock the island-construction tools, but saving yourself a little room in the beginning will save you trouble later on.

■ Don't stop shaking! You'll be shaking lots of trees in New Horizons, especially in the beginning of the game. When a branch falls, don't take that as a sign to stop. Trees will drop eight branches in total, provided the ground below it is clear of weeds and other objects.

■ One of the first DIY recipes that you'll learn is for a simple DIY workbench. It's a good idea to build a couple of these as soon as you can. We recommend placing one near your plaza, and one inside your tent or house. That way, you don't have to keep running inside the residential-services building to use Tom Nook's workbench. You'll find DIY recipes for better-looking benches, so don't worry if you think having a tree stump inside your home is a little tacky. You can replace that bench later.

Have the Nooks been holding out on us?

If you didn't think to look, you might not see important items, such as this slingshot recipe!

■ The Nooks have more items to sell than you might initially think. When you interact with them in the resident-services tent before they get their own store, you can press the R button to open another item tab. There, you can find some great early game recipes, such as a slingshot and collections of other DIY furniture. Once they open the Nook's Cranny store, pressing R when you're interacting with their cabinet will display an array of wallpaper and flooring. It's easy to miss these options, especially if you don't know to look for them.

Nook Miles Upgrades

Nook Miles are one of the most interesting elements of New Horizons. Think of them as both an in-game achievement system and an alternate form of currency. You're rewarded with miles for doing things that you'd normally do, such as catching fish, talking to your animal neighbors, and selling items at the store. At first, the only thing you can spend those miles on is paying Tom Nook back for his island getaway package. Once you've repaid that loan with 5,000 miles, some additional options are available to you.

You can see those additional Nook Mile benefits by interacting with the kiosk inside the resident-services building. There are a fair number of them in the beginning, and you might not know which ones to prioritize. While it's ultimately up to you, we do have a recommended path to take, which will ensure that you're getting the most useful benefits early on and saving the less necessary ones for later.

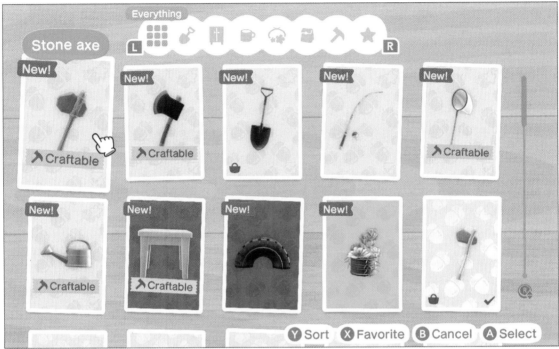

Upgraded tools start with the flimsy versions, so building them is a two-step process.

1. Pretty Good Tools Recipes (3,000 Nook Miles)

Let's face it – you probably weren't instilled with confidence when every tool that you crafted was described as "flimsy." This upgrade isn't cheap, but it lets you build stronger versions of the basic suite of tools. Just to put that in perspective, the flimsy fishing rod will snap after 10 fish are caught. The upgraded version is three times as strong, letting you catch 30 fish before going kaput.

2. Pocket Organization Guide (5,000 Nook Miles)

Your villager's carrying capacity is only 20 slots when you begin your vacation. That's not bad, but you can do better. This upgrade adds another row of 10 slots, meaning that you can go fishing, foraging, or bug-hunting longer without having to sell or drop items on the ground to make room..

It never seems like you have enough space. This upgrade helps.

3. Tool Ring: It's Essential (800 Nook Miles)

This one's slightly less essential when you realize that you can swap between tools by pressing left and right on the Switch's directional pad. Still, it's handy to press up on your Switch's d-pad and quickly jump to a favorite tool rather than cycling through them one by one.

This quick-select menu makes swapping between tools a breeze!

4. Nook Miles Ticket (2,000 Nook Miles)

Tom Nook gives you one of these at no cost, but after that you'll need to pay your own airfare if you want to check out one of New Horizons' other islands. We'll get into those a little later, but it's not a bad idea to pick up a couple extra.

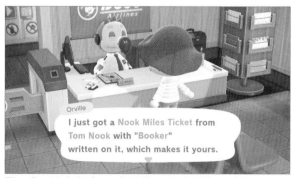

The first trip's free, but the rest will cost you.

Once you fully expand your haircut options…

Those are the biggest priorities, but there are some other things to pick up. If you're into styling your villager, picking up the additional hair colors and styles isn't a bad choice. Keep in mind that you'll need to have access to a mirror or vanity to change your character's appearance, though. The Custom Design Pro Editor is another solid pick, but, like the hair options, it's more of a cosmetic upgrade than anything that will directly affect your gameplay.

Later on, once you upgrade the Resident Services building to a more permanent structure, you can spend your miles on the Ultimate Pocket Stuffing item, which costs 8,000 miles. That upgrades your inventory to its final size of 40 slots. Needles to say, that's another high-priority upgrade, though it won't be available for some time.

… you can come up with some interesting combinations.

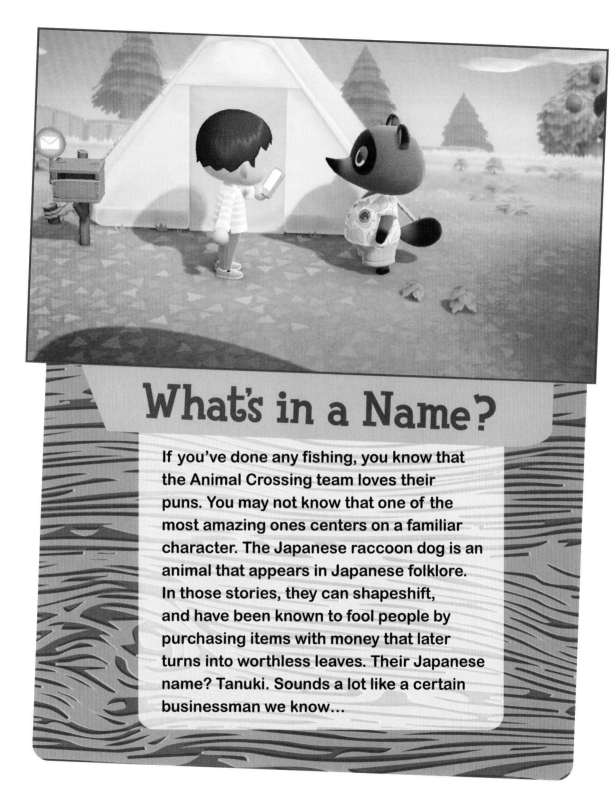

What's in a Name?

If you've done any fishing, you know that the Animal Crossing team loves their puns. You may not know that one of the most amazing ones centers on a familiar character. The Japanese raccoon dog is an animal that appears in Japanese folklore. In those stories, they can shapeshift, and have been known to fool people by purchasing items with money that later turns into worthless leaves. Their Japanese name? Tanuki. Sounds a lot like a certain businessman we know...

Making Money
(and Getting Miles)

There's a reason that Tom Nook has become a meme. His cute exterior and friendly demeanor mask a ruthless, cold-hearted businessman. OK, perhaps that's a little extreme. Let's put it this way: Upgrading your house is one of the core elements of Animal Crossing, and the only way you're going to be able to do so is by dealing with Mr. Nook.

Be careful when you plant trees. When they're too close, it can be tricky to see fossils.

Tom will take your Nook Miles in the beginning of the game, but that changes after he replaces your tent with a more permanent house. From there, he's only interested in bells. Because of that, earning money is something you should keep in the back of your mind. You don't need to be a relentless bell-making machine; after all, this is meant to be a relaxing experience. But unless you're satisfied with life in a one-room house, making money is eventually going to become important. Fortunately, there are plenty of options at your disposal.

Fruit

Your island starts out with its own native fruit variety. Every few days, fruit trees will grow three pieces of fruit, which you can shake down, collect, and then sell. The Nooks don't appear to be too

Only the axe – not the flimsy axe or stone axe – will chop down trees.

impressed with the starter fruit, offering a measly 100 bells apiece. It's better than nothing, but only marginally so.

A few days after you start, you'll receive some additional fruit, which is different from your native fruit. You can certainly sell those to the Nooks – getting 500 bells a pop in the process – but that's a sucker's game. Instead, you should dig a hole with your shovel and plant the fruit.

After a few days, it will grow, and then eventually bear fruit of its own.

There are five different types of fruit to collect – Apples, Cherries, Oranges, Peaches, and Pears – and it's possible to have all types in your village. The easiest way is to find friends who are playing and visit their towns. Bring some of your native fruit, and you can have an exchange. Be sure to ask before shaking

This replanting effort takes time and patience, but you'll reap the rewards.

their trees, though. It's only polite. There are a couple of other plants you can acquire, too: palm trees and bamboo. Both can be found on island visits.

What we like to do is to replace all of the normal trees on our island with fruit trees. It takes quite a while to chop them all down, but it's worth it for a few reasons. First, you get a ton of wood, softwood, and hardwood, which are crafting materials used in the majority of DIY recipes. Next, it's an easy way to ensure that your island isn't overly cluttered with trees, since you're just replacing the existing ones. Finally, it's a pretty lucrative project, when it's completed. You can easily net 100,000 bells or more every harvest day, which only takes a few minutes of shaking and collecting.

Money Trees!

Money doesn't grow on trees, or so the saying goes. That's not exactly true in Animal Crossing. Every day, a random spot on your island will glow gold. Digging in that location will earn you a quick 1,000 bells. Not bad! Don't fill it in, though! You can replant that bag of bells, and it will then sprout into a tree. When full grown, it will bear three bags of cash, each worth 1,000 bells. It gets better, too.

This seems like a weird thing to do, but trust us.

If you like the way money trees look, don't shake them! The bags of bells won't grow back.

If you have the cash to spare, you can select your bell balance on the inventory screen by pressing A. That will allow you to take some of your money and put it into a bag of bells. Choose the 10,000 bell bag, and bury that in the hole. Voila! Soon, you'll triple that amount!

Regardless of how much you deposit, this trick only works once. After that, it turns into an ordinary tree.

Digging holes in these spots will let you get the most from each rock.

Money Rocks!

You've probably noticed those big rocks that are scattered around your island. You can hit them with a shovel or axe to harvest minerals including stone, clay, iron nuggets, and, rarely, gold nuggets. They're all important materials for DIY. You can get up to eight chunks of material from every rock per day, but there's a catch: You have to hit them

Don't ask how these got here. And yes, the sounds are from Super Mario Bros.

Gold nuggets will rarely drop from regular rocks. They're worth 10,000 bells apiece, but it's a good idea to save them for DIY projects.

quickly, and every time you swing your tool you get knocked back a bit. Unless you dig some strategically placed holes or put some furniture in the right spot, you'll only get seven items.

In addition to those boring rocks, one of the rocks on your island is special. Hitting that one will earn you piles of bells, starting with 100 bells and incrementally increasing until the eighth and final sack of 8,000. All told, you can earn an easy 16,100 bells by hitting that rock. It's not going to make you wealthy, but it's a nice windfall for very little effort.

Some fish will only come out in the early morning or late at night.

Fishing and Bug Collecting

Unlike the other methods that we've covered, fishing and bug collecting are activities that can be done repeatedly until you're done. You don't need to wait three days for new fish to appear in your pond. You think bugs only creep on over once a day? Forget about it! You can make as much money as you want with your fishing rod or net, provided you have the time.

There are too many varieties of fish and bugs to cover in this section. Plus, many of them are tied to specific months of the year, times of day, weather conditions, locations, and more. Part of the fun here is discovering what's out there. That said, there are a few rules of thumb to make your life a little more lucrative.

You'll catch more sea bass than you'd ever want to, but sometimes you pull up exciting (and valuable) fish.

When fishing, try to go for the larger shadows. Some smaller varieties have good resale value, but by and large, the bigger, the better. Fishing in the ocean or along rivers is faster than dipping a line in a pond, because of the way the fish spawn into the world. You can walk up and down a beach or riverbed, catching everything you see. With ponds, you have to walk fairly far away from the water for a fresh catch to appear. Ideally, you want to swing by ponds as part of a longer river route.

There are too many variables to give an exact idea of how lucrative fishing can be. With a maxed-out inventory of 40 slots, even a bad hour of fishing can earn you about 100,000 bells. Of course, that can vary wildly depending on your luck. Some fish sell for thousands of bells. Catch a few of those in a row, and you'll be flush. Well, at least you will be until you upgrade your house again.

It's too early here for this trick to work, but this is what a bamboo island looks like during the day.

There's a particularly lucrative way to make money with bugs, but it requires some serious planning. First, wait until after 7 p.m., and then take a plane to one of the random island adventures. If you're lucky, you'll land on a bamboo island. Optimally, it'll be raining. Cut down every bamboo plant, dig up its roots, pick every flower, and break every rock. Once it's clear, dig some holes in a U shape. Those will be your traps.

The goal here is to spawn in some of the big-ticket bugs, either tarantulas or scorpions, depending on the time of year. They're aggressive and will sting you, so be fast. When they chase you, lure them over to where you dug the holes. They won't be able to jump across it, making it easy to snag them with your net without having to worry about getting stung. Each one of these critters is worth 8,000 bells, so you can imagine how much cash you can make on a successful outing.

As long as there's a hole between
you and your prey, you're safe.

Oh, these puns.

Turnips take up a lot of space. Keep them in your house or a fenced-in place outside, so people can't steal them in multiplayer.

Turnips, Turnips, Turnips

This is the big one. The turnip market is another longtime element of Animal Crossing. It sounds weird, but it's easy. Every Sunday morning from 5 a.m. until noon, a wandering NPC named Daisy Mae will come to your island. She's the granddaughter of Joan, who founded Sow Joan's Stalk Market. Yes, the pun game is strong.

Anyway, she'll sell you turnips in bunches of 10, which you can sell to the Nooks for a profit – or a loss –

Daisy Mae

Well, I'll be here every Sunday mornin' with a fresh crop of turnips, so come say hi anytime!

The initial purchase price can vary a little, too, but it's not quite as important as the price the Nooks will pay for them later.

throughout the following week. The Nooks will adjust their buying price twice a day, from when they open until noon, and then noon until their store closes for the day. If this is all new to you, it's not as complicated as it might sound. Long story short, buy a bunch of turnips, and then check in with the Nooks twice a day. Hopefully, they'll buy them at a higher price than what you paid, giving you a nice bit of profit from the transaction.

It's not a risk-free endeavor, but it's also not as risky as it once was. Thanks to the game's popularity and the ease of online play, it's easier than ever to sell turnips and make money. You see, you can visit other peoples' islands and sell there if

their Nooks are buying at a high price. There are several subreddits where people post their turnip prices. Be sure to read the specific posts on the exact etiquette to follow, if you decide that sounds like something you'd like to try. In general, tips are appreciated.

The turnip markets follow a pattern, too. They might be hard for novices to figure out, but several sites allow you to input your daily prices and will recommend when to sell. We recommend visiting www.artem66.github.io/acnh_turnips for its ease of use and accuracy. If you're lucky, it's possible to make a profit of more than 2,000,000 bells with a full 40-slot inventory of turnips. You can also lose big, too, but nobody said the turnip game was easy.

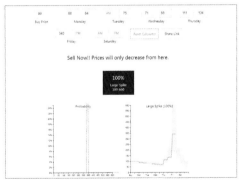

It's not much to look at but this turnip calculator takes away all the guesswork.

Making Friends
(and Improvements)

Animal Crossing is a community sim, and making friends is a big part of the experience – unless it's not. Like the rest of the game, New Horizons is about finding your own bliss. If that means getting to know each of the animal inhabitants on your island, more power to you. Or if you just want to say hello to them as you head toward your favorite fishing spot, that's fine, too.

phoebe

We all just met, but chillin' by the fire like this makes it feel like we've been best buds for ages, sparky.

Whether or not you choose to make friendship a priority, it's important to know the basics. After all, increasing your island's population is an important step toward unlocking some of the most interesting tools in the game. Here are some of the ways you can do that, and what you can do once new residents arrive.

Humble Beginnings

When you begin your island staycation, you're joined with a pair of fellow vacationers. Your island can support up to 10 villagers in total, but you'll have to do a fair amount of work to reach that population cap. Think of those first two as freebies.

After that, you can be proactive. The easiest way to get new residents is to recruit them yourself. You know those Nook Miles Tickets that you can buy from the resident-services kiosk? Use them at the Dodo Airlines airport to visit a random island (tell them "I wanna fly!"). There's a good chance that you won't be alone. Talk to the animal on the island twice, and you'll be able to ask them to move to your island. Of course, if you're not into that animal's particular vibe, you're under no obligation to invite them.

The first time you do this, Tom Nook will give you a pretty big assignment: set aside plots of land for three homes, and furnish their interiors and exteriors. Get ready to spend some time at the DIY workbench, and hopefully you have a lot of resources stockpiled. Nook will give you the recipes for each of the items these houses require, which you then drop off into their assigned boxes.

Your newly recruited villager will move into one of those lots, leaving a couple of extra spots. Repeat the same island process to fill those lots. Once they're booked, Tom Nook realizes that your island isn't just a fly-by-night kind of operation. He'll upgrade the resident-services tent into a full-fledged building, bringing fan-favorite Isabelle along as a special adviser. Some new options will appear in the Nook Miles terminal, including the Ultimate Pocket Stuffer, which will max out your inventory slots.

Tom will then recruit you to build a campsite. This new location will attract a random camper the day after it's built, with a small chance to attract new visitors on subsequent days. To get them to move in, you'll first have to buy a lot from Tom Nook, for 10,000 bells. As long as there's available room, animals seem completely into the concept of island life.

The campsite also lets you use Animal Crossing amiibo cards to attract specific villagers. To do so, you interact with the Nook kiosk, and they'll appear in your campsite. Unlike the animals you encounter in the wild, these guys don't just move in. Instead, you have to repeat the process for several consecutive

days. They might have you craft special DIY objects for them, too, which can be a potentially expensive proposition.

These plots and homes take up a lot of real estate, which means you're probably going to be traveling all over your island. Fortunately, the upgraded residential-services building allows you to build bridges and inclines to make navigation easier. You can choose either one bridge or incline each day, and the prices start at 98,000 bells. Only the Island Representative can choose where

to place these, though other players can contribute to the fund once the space has been allotted. Once the money has been raised, the structure will be ready the following day.

Stinky

I just wanted you to have a cardigan-shirt combo.

Clothes are always appreciated, though don't expect every gift to fit your personal style.

It Pays to Be Friendly

Getting on a villager's good side is pretty easy, since everyone already starts out on friendly terms. That's not to say that your friendships can't improve. Each villager has a hidden friendship meter, which can be improved over time by doing some basic things. Talking to them each day, giving them wrapped presents, and sending them letters will improve your relationships. Eventually, they'll start giving you gifts, will ask you to help think of new catchphrases, and ultimately send you a framed autographed portrait. It's a nice bonus, though admittedly it's not something that every player needs to collect.

Stinky

Wanna try Reactions for yourself?
Just hit [ZR]. Do enough and BAM!
There's your stretches for the day!

You'll be able to collect more than 40 different reactions over time!

Framed portraits aside, interacting with your villagers can get you some other fun things. One of the most fun collectibles they can give you are the reactions, which are Animal Crossing's version of emotes. They're a silly way to do things like express surprise or joy, act shocked, or even sneeze. They're particularly fun when playing with actual friends via online multiplayer.

This character from your dream plays a big role in the game.

Final Steps

Once you have a bustling island, you're within range of New Horizon's final step – or as close to one as the game gets. Your goal is to improve the island's star ranking, which you can get by talking to Isabelle. Plant flowers, pick up weeds and debris, and set out objects that look nice, and you'll be on your way to attracting the attention of another longtime fan favorite, K.K. Slider.

Tom Nook is a big fan of this talented pup. Once you get Mr. Slider to visit, he'll put on a special show for the island.

This app changes everything. For real.

Better still, he'll make it part of his weekly tour schedule, appearing after 6 p.m. every Saturday. In those shows, he takes requests, too!

After the first concert, Tom Nook shows his appreciation by adding another app to your Nook Phone: the Island Designer.

This is the big one! It lets you dig waterways, add to cliff faces or shave them down, and ultimately shape the island the way you want. We'll get into some of that in a little while.

Maximizing Your Fun

Chores can be kind of fun. It sounds a little counterintuitive, but that element of the game is something that many Animal Crossing fans can relate to. Part of the Animal Crossing experience comes down to completing a series of repeating tasks every day. There are a lot of things to keep track of, especially if you're a new player. With that in mind, here's a rundown of some of the things you can – and probably should – be doing every day that you play Animal Crossing: New Horizons.

Water the Plants

If you're growing flowers, it's a good idea to water them every day. They'll show their appreciation by sparkling a little, and they'll also have a chance of producing rare hybrid varieties.

The flimsy watering can only douses the space directly in front of you, but upgraded versions water your plants in a sweeping arc.

Bang the Rocks

There are six rocks on your island, so be sure to hit each one every day with an axe or shovel. You'll get tons of resources, and also a little bit of extra cash from the money rock.

Remember to dig a hole or place objects in these positions, so you can get the most items from each rock!

Find the Fossils

Four fossils will spawn in your island every day. Be sure to dig them up and have Blathers identify them for you at the museum. Whether you choose to donate them or sell them is up to you, but you can't do either one if you leave them buried.

Don't get bamboozled! Bamboo shoots have the same ground pattern as fossils, but Blathers isn't interested in them.

Look! I dug up
1,000 Bells!

Find the Money Spot

We already covered this, too, but keep an eye out for the glowing golden spot on the ground. It's an easy way to get 1,000 bells, and you can earn more in the long term if you plant a bag of bells into it.

There's only one money spot on your island each day, so keep your eyes peeled!

Collect Fruit

Is there any fruit hanging around? Shake it down and sell it! Or, if you're feeling generous, mail it to some of your villagers. They seem to appreciate it.

It's not a bad idea to collect the less-valuable native fruit for eating, so you can dig up grown trees and break rocks when it's landscaping time.

Comb the Beach

Shells aren't generally a lucrative resource, but it's not a bad idea to collect them all at least once a day. Also, keep an eye out for messages inside bottles. They usually contain DIY recipes, and you can never have too many of those…

Shells aren't worth much, but at least they stack in your inventory to take up less space.

Bruce

Howdy! I'm just stakin' a claim for a bit, enjoyin' the campin' life. Be seein' you around, gruff!

Look for Visitors

More and more visitors will swing by your island as it grows, and it's a good idea to meet up with them if you can. We'll get into the specifics soon, but ultimately you should always say hi to strangers in New Horizons.

Tired of waiting for guests? Use an amiibo to bring in specific animal friends.

Tommy

The current price for turnips is 143 Bells per turnip!

Check Turnip Prices

This is another must if you're investing in the turnip market. Prices change at noon, so try to stay on top of the market before and after that time. You never know when it may surge from 100 bells to 600 or more – and you'd hate to miss out on that opportunity.

You win some, you lose some. Oh well.

🛒 Nook Shopping		4,520
👉 🌿 Cypress plant		🪙 1,000
🌿 Outdoor table		🪙 2,200
🧢 Rain hat		🪙 880
👓 Oval glasses		🪙 880
👕 Hi tee		🪙 640
👕 Six-ball tee		🪙 560
👖 Denim skirt		🪙 1,120
👟 Slip-on loafers		🪙 490
🎵 Surfin' K.K.		🪙 3,200

🪙 1,000

Ⓑ Sign Off   Ⓐ Select

Buy Catalog Items

You can only buy five things from the Nook Catalog every day, and it's a good habit to get into. Buy the cheapest things you can find, and, if you're into music, pick up the K.K. Slider tune while you're at it. The selection rotates daily, and your loyalty will eventually pay off with a Nook Phone app that lets you shop via your handheld device.

Check the Recycling

There's a recycling container next to the counter in the island-services center, and its contents are up for grabs. It's usually full of things you may not need, such as saplings or cardboard boxes, but occasionally you'll find clothing and interesting crafting materials inside. It's worth making it part of your daily routine.

The box almost always has cardboard boxes inside.

Timmy

Seems like you're interested in a garbage bin.

Check the Shops

Speaking of shopping, check the inventory of your shops every day. They rotate, too, and you never know what's going to be available.

Mabel

That mannequin is looking pretty stylish, isn't it? Anything in particular catch your eye?

The Able Sisters' shelf items rotate daily, but the outfits on mannequins stick around for several days – for better, or worse.

Should I toss something?

Taking Out the Trash

Not everything you catch is worth keeping. That's something you'll soon learn while fishing. In addition to fish, there's a small chance you'll snag empty cans, boots, tires, and stones. You'll get a few DIY recipes for collecting enough of them, but ultimately they just take up space. For that reason, we like to keep a garbage can near our fishing routes. That way, you don't waste inventory space hauling trash around, and you don't litter, either.

Important Characters and Places

Between fishing, cultivating plants, designing clothes, and that whole "building up a town from nothing" thing, you're one busy person! You're not the only one who has a lot on their plate, however. Many of the villagers and visitors have special reasons for being on your island. Some will offer you amazing things to buy, while others may offer valuable services. It's a lot to keep track of, so let's talk about some of the notable places and faces you'll be interacting with during your time on the island.

Tom Nook

All told, we'll be looking at a grand total of 2,498,000 Bells. Are you still interested?

Tom Nook's valuable services don't come cheap.

Tom Nook

Tom Nook is the head honcho of Animal Crossing: New Horizons. After all, he's the one who set up your island getaway package in the first place. He can be found in the resident-services tent, which is later upgraded to a full-fledged building. If you want to build a house or upgrade your dwelling, you're going to have to go through him. He also sends you new apps for your Nook Phone periodically. Basically, he's the conduit through which just about every improvement in the game goes through. Best of all, he doesn't seem to need sleep, since his services are available 24/7.

Nook's Cranny starts small, but it expands after about a month or so.

Timmy and Tommy Nook

Tom Nook may be in charge, but Timmy and Tommy do their part to help their mentor succeed. The pair buy and sell items to the player, first from the resident-services tent and later from their very own store, Nook's Cranny. The store is small at first, but it expands to showcase more items. The inventory rotates every day, so it's worth stopping in to see what's on offer. Hours are 8 a.m. to 10 p.m. seven days a week. They do have a drop-off box outside the store if you want to sell items outside of business hours. It's not a great deal, however; that service only pays 80 percent of what you'd normally get, and the money comes by mail the next day.

Blathers will give you a short lecture on everything you donate to the museum.

Blathers and the Museum

This friendly owl comes to your town after you donate enough fish or insects to his research project via Tom Nook. Eventually, he'll establish the largest place you can visit inside New Horizons: the museum. This place is a depository of every insect, fossil, fish, and piece of art you've donated to his cause. The more you give, the more interesting it becomes. Even if you aren't feeling generous, Blathers is happy to identify fossils for you. Blathers is nocturnal, so you'll have to wake him up first if you visit during the day. At night, he's already awake and ready to go. It's a fun little detail that's easy to miss. His sister, Celeste, will sometimes visit at night, too. Talk to her, and she'll teach you about constellations and falling stars.

Blathers hates bugs,
but his professionalism
allows him to set up fairly
intricate displays.

Different ecosystems
have their own areas,
including freshwater
and saltwater tanks.

The museum is empty
at first, but it will fill
up over time with your
help.

Blathers only displays
the real deal in his
art wing, so don't
try to pass off any
forgeries.

Isabelle wants to help you bring the island up to its full potential.

Isabelle

Isabelle is another important member of Tom Nook's team. She's in charge of the island's overall image. Once the resident-services building is constructed, you can visit her counter to get your island-evaluation score. If you achieve a five-star rating, you'll get the DIY recipe for a gold watering can! She can also help you change your town's musical theme and flag, and also help with a few villager tasks. For instance, if you've given clothing to a villager and you don't like the way it looks, she can send a hint to that villager to revert back to their default clothing. She won't, however, let you kick anyone out.

Orville maintains the operations back home....

... while Wilbur takes to the skies.

Orville, Wilbur, and the Airport

Don't call these dodos "flightless." Orville and Wilbur are in charge of the skies in New Horizons. Orville can be found at the airport counter, where he's in charge of booking travel. Whether you want to take a mystery-island tour, visit a friend, or have other players visit you, you'll need to talk to him. He also helps out with the mail, letting you send mail (and optional gifts) to friends and villagers. Wilbur operates the plane. He also sells basic tools, in case your gear breaks while you're on a mystery tour. All in all, these guys are worthy of their namesakes.

You'd think he'd be better at sailing – or staying on his ship – by now.

Gulliver

The first time you spot Gulliver washed up on the beach, it's an alarming sight. Don't worry, he's fine. You just need to talk to him several times to wake him up. Once he's alert, he'll realize his phone is broken so he can't call in a rescue. You can help by digging up five communicator parts on the beach. Look for the waterspouts that usually signal a clam is around. After retrieving and returning them to Gulliver, he'll send out an S.O.S. beacon. The next day, you'll get rewarded for your help with a special item. The can including clothing, furniture, and decorations. They're all themed to different cultures around the world, which is only fitting considering his traveling lifestyle.

Redd

> Well, well! You from around here?
> Hi, the name's Redd. I work in sales.
> And you are...

Redd seems friendly, but you should be careful before giving him any of your hard-earned bells.

Jolly Redd

In previous Animal Crossing games, this fox was known as Crazy Redd. Now he's taken on the name Jolly Redd. Regardless of what you call him, his shady dealings have remained consistent. He sells paintings on his tiny ship, which will dock on your island's northern beach. They seem like a great way to fill up the museum's art wing, but beware: Some, if not most, of the art items he's hawking are actually forgeries. If you try to donate them to Blathers, you'll realize how worthless your purchase was. Fortunately, there are usually telltale signs as to the items' authenticity. Most of his art is well known, so examine it against a picture of the original to find any discrepancies.

Everything seems fine on his ship, but be sure to take a closer look at the items.

Zooming in on a painting may reveal details that aren't quite right...

... Such as the eyebrows on this Mona Lisa forgery. Nice try, Redd!

Support small businesses, and help them grow!

Mabel, Sabel, and Label

These fashion-conscious sisters will help you get on the right side of fashion. Mabel will first visit right after Nook's Cranny is built. She'll sell you a few clothing items when she visits, ultimately deciding to stick around more permanently. Once you build the Able Sisters store, they'll sell a wide range of outfits from 9 a.m. to 9 p.m. They also operate a kiosk in the back, which lets you download patterns that other players have created. Sabel can be found in the back, sewing, but she's notoriously quiet. Label is the wanderer of the family, popping up from time to time to give players fashion challenges. You can't really fail these, but it's worth participating for the free duds. Kicks isn't a member of the family (he's a skunk), but he also sells hard-to-find clothes and bags when he visits. Look for him in the plaza.

19,660

Saharah

Hello. You are calling me Saharah, for it is the name I have carried for as long as I have carried these rugs.

This camel's wares are one of a kind!

Saharah

Saharah is another fixture in the Animal Crossing series. She travels the world, selling special wallpapers, flooring, and rugs. You don't know what you'll get when you buy mystery wallpapers and flooring (it is a mystery, after all), but that's where you can get some of the coolest decorative items for your home.

They include special rare wallpapers that feature animated thunderstorm, aquarium, surveillance-camera footage, and more. You also get special tickets for patronizing her shop, which can be redeemed for freebies.

> Harvey
>
> I wanna learn from your example and make my island, like, the perfect artists' collective.

Harvey may be a little weird, but he's a boon for photo buffs!

Harvey and His Island

This wandering hippie is about one thing: photography. Once you meet this wandering shutterbug, you'll be able to fly out to his island (ask for "Harv's Island" at the airport). There, you can set up photoshoots with your villagers, pose them, and add props. Once you've recruited a villager for a session, you'll be able to buy a poster of that villager back home through Nook Shopping.

> Harvey
>
> Just hit the airport and tell 'em you want to go to Harv's Island. That's the name of my pad. Groovy, right?

Daisy is taking over duties for her grandmother, Joan.

Daisy Mae

Daisy is the key to one of the best ways of making money in Animal Crossing. She sells turnips every Sunday morning until noon, which can be resold at (fingers crossed) a profit at Nook's Cranny.

C.J.

I have this feelin'...like someone's gonna reel in the big one, and then I'll get to talk about it on my show!

This beaver has a passion for fishing!

CJ & Flick

CJ and Flick are two wandering travelers who are worth looking out for. CJ has a fishing show, and he'll offer special challenges for would-be anglers. With his leather jacket and punk styling, chameleon Flick isn't trying to blend in. He's all about the bugs. The visitors will make you trophies of either fish or insects, provided you give them three of the same type. Better still, they pay a premium for their favorite critters – a whopping 150-percent higher normal selling price. For that reason, it's worth hanging onto the rare fish and bugs you find so you can cash in when these guys visit.

If you want plants, Leif is your guy!

Leif

He may be a sloth, but Leif's service is quick. He sells a variety of garden supplies, including flowers and shrubs. If you want to incorporate the natural world into your outdoor decorations, he's a great resource.

This chill musician is always up for a visit.

K.K. Slider

K.K. Slider is one of the first characters you meet in Animal Crossing: New Horizons, even if it's only in a dream. Getting this pup to actually set foot on your island takes a lot more work. Once you eventually lure him to your town, he'll put on a weekly show. Every Saturday, starting at 6 p.m., he'll perform a song for you, sending you a record after the show. He takes requests, too, so put in a song title and see what happens.

Fish (and Make Bait)!

You've undoubtedly seen the little water spouts that appear on the shore. Dig them up, and you can get a clam – which can then be used to make bait. Making a bunch of bait is tedious, but it's a great way to attract fish that you're looking for in specific locations, such as near the pier, in ponds, or the mouths of rivers.

Expressing Yourself

When it comes to player expression, it's hard to beat Animal Crossing. New Horizons takes the series' foundational sense of freedom and goes even further with it. In past installments, you had control over your character and house – and fans lost countless hours finding ways to show off their creativity. New Horizons gives you close to total free rein over your island. Want a new pond? You can dig one yourself. Not happy with the way a river winds around your town? Shape it to your specifications. There's a lot of power at your fingertips, once you learn how to wield it.

Mirrors work inside or out – go figure.

Who Do You Want to Be?

When you first start New Horizons, you begin by taking your passport photo. It's a clever way of guiding you through character creation, but that's far from the only opportunity you'll have to shape the way you look. Over the course of the first few days, you'll get some new clothing and, if you're lucky, access to a mirror.

Mirrors are great, because they allow you to return to the character creation and tweak your appearance all over again. Didn't like the eyes you picked? Not happy with a haircut? You can change any of that simply by interacting with the mirror. Similarly, clothing can be easily changed by picking the item and selecting "wear" from your inventory.

Once you upgrade your tent to an actual house, you'll be able to store items

Mabel

A pacifier?

Before you buy something from the sisters…

in your house's inventory – including clothing. A variety of different pieces of furniture, such as wardrobes and even refrigerators can be interacted with, and will allow you to piece together outfits by clothing type. It's a lot easier to manage than having to pull out individual articles of clothing, moving them to your inventory, and putting them on.

The Able Sisters sell a huge array of clothing, much of which rotates in and out daily. They only show off a tiny selection of what they have on hand at any given time, so be sure to enter the fitting room to see everything that's available. It's a good idea to check that fitting room before picking up an item, since items are often available in colors, patterns, and other variations than the one on display.

If you aren't impressed with the clothes that you can buy, you can create your

... check out the fitting room.

own patterns and wear them around. Your Nook Phone has a design app on it, and you can spend your Nook Miles on the pro design patterns. These are particularly cool because they give you more control over your patterns than in previous Animal Crossings.

Each of the pro patterns can be designed around a specific article of clothing. Rather than creating a simple design that's stretched across shirts, dresses, and flags, these pro designs factor in the unique aspects of each piece of clothing. You can make a baseball cap, for example, with special detailing on the brim, front, and back.

Perhaps you want to be fashionable, but aren't able to execute an idea to your satisfaction. Keep trying! In the meantime, it's easy to find the creations that other users have shared and bring them into your game, provided you

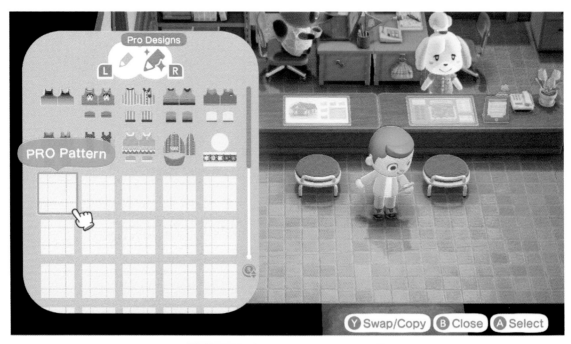

have a subscription to Nintendo Online. The easiest way is to search online for "Animal Crossing design ID codes." Use those at the kiosk in the back of the Able Sisters to import them into your game. If you have a mobile device, you can download the Nintendo Online app, which will allow you to use your device's camera to import patterns into your game via QR codes. Those can also be easily found online, such as on the Animal Crossing QR Code subreddit (reddit.com/r/acqr).

Whether you like carefully designed spaces…

… or want to show off your eclectic side, it's up to you!

Closer to Home

The first few weeks you spend on your island can be intimidating. You do your best to buy interesting items from shops, and villagers give you random furniture. But when it comes time to decorate your house, it looks like a thrift store exploded. Don't worry! While it can be a little tricky to come up with a home that looks presentable – if that's your goal – it's absolutely within reach. In fact, you start out with virtually everything you need.

A few days after you start playing, Tom Nook will offer you a tutorial on customization. This is an additional layer on top of the existing DIY process, allowing you to take an item of furniture and, well, customize it a bit. That can be something as simple as changing its color, to being able to swap out the sheets on a bed from several presets – or even apply your own designs.

Here's a quick rundown on what you can do with DIY recipes that you can access from the first few days of play. Let's start by crafting a set of wooden furniture.

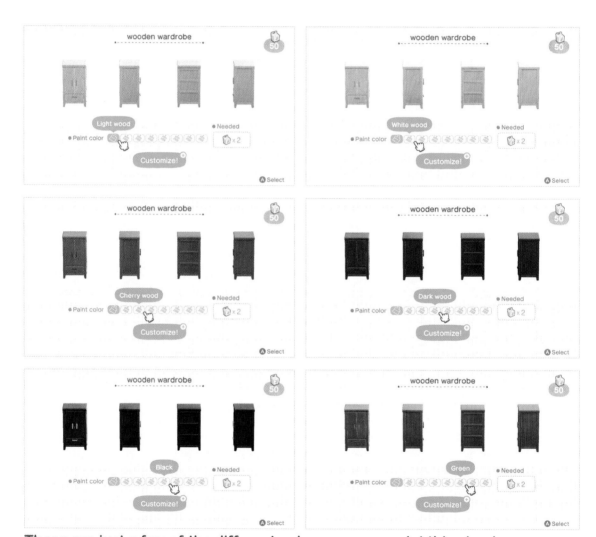

These are just a few of the different colors you can paint this simple wardrobe.

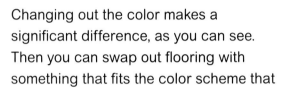

Changing out the color makes a significant difference, as you can see. Then you can swap out flooring with something that fits the color scheme that

you have in mind. Adding a few simple props, such as a sofa, plant, clock, and homework on the desk, makes it feel more like a lived-in home.

Don't forget the walls, either. We found this corkboard in Nook's Cranny, and it was a perfect addition to our little homework nook. Even if you don't have all the items necessary to make your dream home, it's possible – and satisfying – to make the most of what's available.

Tom Nook can upgrade your house several times, adding three new rooms on the ground floor, as well as an upper floor and basement. Along the way, he'll also allow you to tweak more of your home's exterior, including the roof color, door, mailbox, and siding. While it's easy to obsess over the interior, don't forget to pay attention to your home's outward appearance!

Flower Power

When you first get the watering-can recipe from Tom Nook, he tells you something about how watering plants daily can give you specially colored hybrids. That little nugget of information comes during a particularly busy part of your early island life, and it's easy to forget about it. It's worth a quick refresher, especially if you enjoy plants or want to conduct some botany experiments. For real.

First you need to buy some seeds, either from the Nooks or the visiting plant vendor, Leif. Plant them in staggered rows, leaving a space between each plant. Think of it like a checkerboard pattern. Water them daily, and you'll

see little sparkles appear on them. Eventually, they'll sprout. Once they bloom, consistently watered plants will have a chance to create hybrid colors, based on the flowers that are nearby.

For example, two white hyacinths that are close to each other stand a chance of creating a blue variation. Or, two red tulips can create a black tulip. Roses are particularly complicated. To make blue hybrids, you first need to create a hybrid between purple and red blooms, to make a hybrid pink variant. That hybrid pink is

used with a yellow rose to make a hybrid red. Finally, two hybrid reds can make a blue rose.

Part of the fun comes from experimentation. The color variations in New Horizon are based on Mendelian genetics, with dominant and recessive traits affecting the colors that a flower's offspring can take on. It's fascinating stuff, and a lot of fun to play around with. All it takes is seeds, a watering can, and some patience.

Shaping the World Around You

As we've said before, the Island Designer app changes everything. It takes a while before Tom Nook trusts you with the ability to reshape the island, but it's absolutely worth the wait.

When you first get it, you're only able to lay out paths. It's a handy tool for making cosmetic tweaks to your island, and it can go a long way toward making your town an easy-to-navigate destination. Make paths between your key points of interest, design signage, and visitors will have an easy time figuring out where to go. After all, their islands are different.

The real power comes with the cliff-construction and waterscaping tools. After you unlock the required permits for these tools (a whopping 6,000 Nook Miles a pop), you can adjust the land to your liking. For example, when we placed the museum, we put it too close to the water's edge – something we warned you about earlier! We could have paid Tom Nook to move the building, but we wanted to wait until we could make the changes by ourselves.

In addition to marking out routes, you can use the pathing tool to simulate flower beds, boardwalks, and other things.

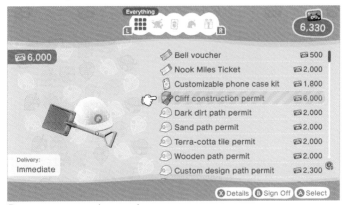

Power comes at a cost, as you can see.

Along similar lines, the cliff-construction tool allows you to notch into the land on cliffsides or build them out further. To demonstrate, we coaxed a little peninsula from the side of our cliff – perfect for a potted plant. OK, we may be squandering this ability a little bit.

The best part is that once you unlock these tools, you don't need any other materials; you won't have to carry around bags of dirt or worry about

your inventory filling up with unwanted rocks. If you have the desire (and the patience), you can turn the majority of your island's square footage into a massive pond. It's really up to you!

A few strokes of the shovel, and we've got a walking path!

Sounds Like Town Spirit

We've spent a lot of time here catering to our eyeballs, but let's not forget our ears! There are a couple of ways that you can tweak New Horizons' soundscape. First, you know the little jingle that plays when you enter a store, talk to a villager, or the clock rings in a new hour? If you talk to Isabelle, she'll let you change out your town's tune!

Isabelle
I think the current anthem is a classic, but there's always room for change and improvement!

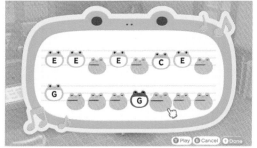

The standard tune is great, but we prefer the classics...

The composition tools are about as simple as it gets. Move the frog heads up and down to play higher or lower notes, adding silence (grayed-out frogs) where necessary. If you can bang out a tune on a xylophone, you'll be set.

Finally, those K.K. Slider albums that you can buy from Nook Shopping or receive from the dog himself have a couple of purposes. First, the album art is generally great, and it's suitable for hanging on your walls. We won't

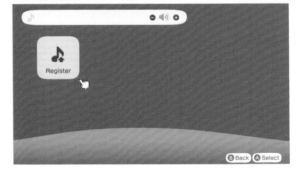

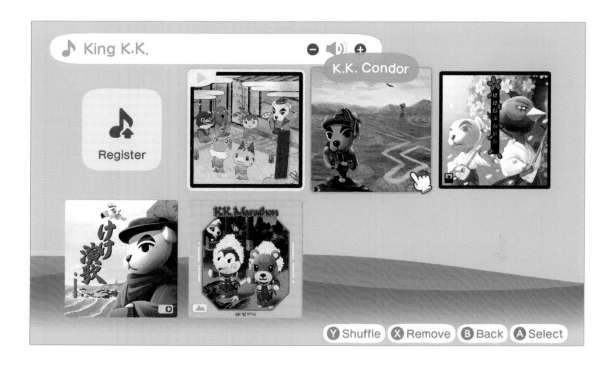

blame you if you decide to decorate your home with some choice cuts – there's a reason he's had a career this long, after all.

Of course, you can actually listen to these things instead. The radio that you get when you first begin the game plays whatever is being "broadcast," but if you purchase a stereo or phonograph, you'll have more control over what you hear. Interact with your device, and you can choose to register

music. Select the albums, and they'll be added to the playlist of available tunes. Unfortunately, it'll consume the album in the process – but you can still check out the album art when you interact with the stereo again.

Events and Activities

Time is of the essence, especially when it comes to Animal Crossing. Even from the very beginning, the series has always been synced to the clock. In a game like Stardew Valley, tasks that take a day to complete do so along with the game's accelerated clock. It's not like that in Animal Crossing. If a character tells you to come back tomorrow, that means, well, to come back tomorrow. Hours take hours, days take days, and weeks take weeks. Fortunately, there are loads of compelling reasons to keep checking in.

We're still early on in Animal Crossing: New Horizons' lifespan, which makes it a particularly exciting time to get into the game. In past entries, events and holidays helped break up the potential monotony of the day-to-day grind. We don't yet have a full picture of what's to come in New Horizons, but judging from the first burst of holiday-themed content, we're confident that there's a lot of great stuff in store.

What Are Holidays Like?

The spring brought players several new themed events and activities. The big one was Bunny Day. This traditional Animal Crossing event spanned April 1-12, and marked the arrival of Zipper T. Bunny. The not-quite-Easter event focused on finding eggs throughout town, by fishing, digging, shaking trees, and popping balloons. These eggs could then be used in special DIY recipes.

A May Day event let players travel to a special island for a shot at solving a hedge maze. It seemed simple, but it required clever use of item management – especially since you weren't allowed to bring any tools with you on the trip. Once solved players got a special gift from Rover, the wandering cat who used to be a big part of earlier Animal Crossing games.

Other big Animal Crossing holidays include Halloween, the Harvest Festival (which is loosely based on Thanksgiving), the Christmas analog Toy Day, and New Year's Day. Although these holidays may be familiar to players, New Horizons is taking a break from tradition in one significant way: The game content isn't built into the game cart or download. Instead, Nintendo has been updating the game with seasonal content. What that boils down to is that players can't access that content ahead of time and get a sneak peek. Yes, we're about to cover one of the most controversial aspects of the game: time travel. Uh oh.

Birthdays naturally only come once a year. That is, unless you meddle with your clock...

Time Travel

Players can be impatient. Waiting for something is a double-edged sword. On one hand, there's a lot of great stuff to collect and build in New Horizons. On the other, you have to wait a long time to earn much of it. For example, the store's inventory only stocks so many items,

and it seems like that pinball machine you need is never going to come into the rotation! What can you do?!

There is an alternative to waiting, but it comes with a few caveats. You know how your Nintendo Switch has a built-in system clock and calendar? That's what New Horizons uses to determine what

Mr. Resetti
was annoying,
but endearing
– you can
even buy
toys of the
character!

time it is in your game. If a person were to close their Animal Crossing game, enter the system menu, and change the date and time to some time in the future, would the game be fooled into thinking the time had passed? Yep! And as of this writing at least, there don't appear to be any significant consequences to doing so. It wasn't always like that.

Players who thought they were clever by messing with the system's clocks in earlier games faced the wrath of Mr. Resetti. This loquacious mole would emerge near a player's home if a player restarted a game without having saved earlier or they tweaked the clock. Then, he'd give a long-winded lecture about the joys of being patient and the satisfaction that comes with taking life one day at a time. The more

Time travelling can used for minor things, such as skipping ahead on rainy days to bring out the sun.

frequently players saw him, the longer these lectures would take. If you thought Blathers could prattle on about bugs or fossils, you have no idea.

Mr. Resetti's temperament relaxed a bit in Animal Crossing: New Leaf. There, he'd still pop up, but you'd have to build a special surveillance center for him if you wanted to see him more than once. In New Horizons, he doesn't have a presence at all. Maybe we'll see him on Groundhog Day? At any rate, you can change your clock without having to worry about a visit from Mr. Resetti at least.

There, that's better…days to bring out the sun.

What other consequences might you face? Well, if you move the clock around too much, weeds will grow in your town again, so you may have to do some mass removal. Animals might possibly move out, which could mean trouble if you like your current living arrangement. Any turnips in your possession will rot, making the investment items worthless. And, we're not joking here, your hair will get messed up after extended periods away from the game. That's some serious bedhead.

Of course, that's subject to change. Nintendo has already adjusted some things inside the game, such as how interest is earned from their ADB accounts. Players were zipping ahead and snagging tens of thousands of bells

Every day can be your birthday, if you'd like it to be.

in interest; the amount you can possibly earn from that scheme now has been reduced. It's possible that Nintendo may take further moves to punish players who time travel, so you do so at your own risk.

While it's not possible to skip ahead to participate in events that haven't yet happened (these holidays aren't yet in the game, after all), you can reverse time to check out the holidays that you may have missed. Want to see Zipper, but didn't get the game until long after he hopped into town? Go for it! Again, just be aware that some weird things may happen by doing so.

	Eventuality	
	Fish	
Accomplished	Grandma	
Animal	Grandpa	
Arrived	Influencer	
City Folk	Island Dweller	
Creative	**Island Resident**	**Confirm** ⊕
Deserted-Island	Lad	
Down-And-Out	Lass	
Festive	Lawn Clippings	
Freshly Delivered	Mama	
Happy Home	Observationist	
Horizon-Bound	Older Brother	

Ⓑ Back

PASSPORT

I love oranges!

🐛 Tabula   🍊 Oranges

Creative Island Resident

Booker

🐾 Born May 1st

👤 Resident Rep.

Reg. April 25th, 2020

‹ ‹ ‹ ‹ ‹ ‹ ‹ ‹ ‹ ‹ ‹ ‹ ‹ ‹ ‹ ‹ ‹ ‹ ‹

 Ⓑ Close   Ⓐ Edit

Don't Forget to Write (Your Title)

There's a side benefit to earning Nook Miles, too! You've probably noticed random words that appear with the milestones. Those can be used to create your official title on your passport. It's a silly thing that's also pretty easy to miss. Access your passport on your Nook Phone, and then edit the title. The more tasks you've completed, the more options you'll have. When you visit other islands in multiplayer, the villagers will remember your title and tell other residents about it. It's a small, strange touch, completely in line with the rest of Animal Crossing.

Animal Crossing Over the Years

Animal Crossing: New Horizons has brought in legions of new fans while satisfying longtime players. In many ways, it's the product of nearly two decades of iteration and steady improvement. There have been missteps during the series' run, to be sure, but New Horizons represents a polished version of what its creators have worked toward all this time.

To fully appreciate how far we've come, it's a good idea to look back and see how we got here. Many of the games we'll cover here are difficult to track down today, but it's good to know what came before. In addition, contemporary fans can continue exploring the world and characters of Animal Crossing – though not necessarily in the way that they might expect. Here's a quick look at Animal Crossing history.

Main Entries

Animal Crossing (GameCube, 2001)

Believe it or not, what would become Animal Crossing started out as a dungeon-crawling adventure game with social elements. Originally slated for the Japan-only Nintendo 64 disk-drive add-on, it was hastily reworked to fit onto a standard N64 cartridge, where the action was removed and the animal interactions became the focus. Later that year, it was ported over to the GameCube and eventually released worldwide. Whew! The GameCube version is crude to look at by today's standards, but it's remarkable how much of it has stuck throughout the series. Some elements, such as the ability to visit islands by connecting a Game Boy Advance to the console, have been updated in New Horizons in the form of mystery tours. Other aspects, such as being able to collect and play retro NES games, have unfortunately been lost.

Animal Crossing: Wild World (Nintendo DS, 2005)

The first Animal Crossing sequel hit Nintendo's portable DS system a few years after the GameCube release, adding some important functionality while paring down a few expected features. Online integration was the big new feature, allowing players to interact and visit other players' towns. The system's second screen was also utilized, giving players a glimpse at the sky without having to move the in-game camera. Unfortunately, the development team eliminated region-specific holidays, removing one of the reasons some players checked in on the game throughout the year.

Animal Crossing: City Folk (Wii, 2008)

City Folk brought the series back to consoles, and Nintendo made up for Wild World's mistakes. Most importantly, holidays made a return. As the title implies, City Folk introduced a new city area that players could travel to. There, they could interact with a variety of shops to buy new clothing and furniture, style their character, and more. Wild World players could transfer their characters over from that game into City Folk, too, which was a fantastic idea. It also supported the Wii Speak microphone peripheral, allowing players to chat with their voices while playing online.

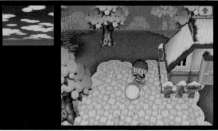

Animal Crossing: New Leaf (Nintendo 3DS, 2012)

New Horizons wasn't the first game in the series to give players a taste of power. In New Leaf, they took on the role of mayor, which gave them the power to set up public-works projects like bridges and buildings. They could also pass ordinances, which had a variety of different effects. Former mayor Tortimer wasn't completely out of the picture; you could visit his island to play minigames with the dapper tortoise. Oddly enough, K.K. Slider had a brief change in musical direction, spinning discs as a nightclub DJ. New Leaf doubled down on customization and player sharing, letting fans share their custom creations via QR codes. It was also the last main release in the series until 2020, with the release of a certain game called Animal Crossing: New Horizons…

Spin-Offs

While the series has had five main entries over the course of its lifespan, that doesn't mean that Nintendo didn't revisit the world of Animal Crossing. There were a few spinoffs that featured familiar characters and elements of the series' town-simulation gameplay, but they're not considered full Animal Crossing games.

Animal Crossing Plaza (Nintendo Wii U, 2013)

Animal Crossing Plaza wasn't really a game, or at least not in the traditional sense. This special version of the Wii U's Miiverse was created as a promotion for New Leaf. Players could download the free software and chat with their fellow Animal Crossing enthusiasts, leave messages and screenshots, and get New Leaf information. Visitors could also swap clothing designs via QR codes.

Animal Crossing: Happy Home Designer (Nintendo 3DS, 2015)

This one was for the decorators out there. Happy Home Designer focused primarily on helping villagers out by remodeling their homes. Customers would show their gratitude by gifting additional pieces of furniture, making more complex projects possible. It supported the collectible Amiibo cards, which let players import their favorite characters into the game. Later, an update to New Leaf would add support for these, too. Happy Home Designer introduced some tweaks to the design interface, such as the ability to move items in half-block increments, but it was a limited experience overall.

Animal Crossing Amiibo Festival (Nintendo Wii U, 2015)

Amiibo Festival was probably the biggest departure that Animal Crossing took from the mainline series. If you've played any of the Mario Party games, you'll know why it's tough not to draw direct comparisons between that series and Amiibo Festival. It was basically a party game, where players rolled a die to advance spaces and play minigames. It had many of the familiar Animal Crossing trappings, but its gameplay was completely different. On the bright side, it was the impetus for several of the Animal Crossing Amiibo figures, which remained charming collectibles long after you stopped playing the game.

Animal Crossing: Pocket Camp (Mobile, 2017)

Consider this camping simulator a predecessor to New Horizons' island getaway. Players weren't able to build up a complete town – roughing it is very much a big part of this mobile title – but it's still a nicely compact version of the Animal Crossing experience. It drew criticism for its reliance on microtransactions, where players could speed up the time it took to craft items or perform some tasks. Some players were concerned that New Horizons would follow suit, which fortunately wasn't the case. Players can link their Pocket Camp and New Horizons accounts, which unlocks special items in the Nook Shopping catalog, too.

More Animal Crossing on Switch

Animal Crossing: New Horizons is great, and going back to some of the earlier entries in the series can be a little rough now. At the same time, we completely understand if you want to play in the Animal Crossing world a little longer. Well, you're in luck! There are a couple of Switch games that have some pretty significant nods to Animal Crossing. And to sweeten the deal, they also happen to be two of the best games on the platform…

Mario Kart 8 Deluxe (2017)

Mario Kart 8 was a standout title on the Wii U, and the Switch version is even better. Mario Kart 8 Deluxe includes all the downloadable content from the original release, including a track based on Animal Crossing and a Villager driver. It's a rip-roaring romp through town, where you can see villagers including Tom Nook and landmarks such as the museum. Of course, the action moves so quickly that you may not be able to fully appreciate all of the details. There are seasonal variations of the track, too, so you can race in spring, summer, fall, and winter.

Super Smash Bros. Ultimate (2018)

We'll admit that it's a little strange to watch Isabelle and a Villager duke it out in combat, but we've been assured that it's all for fun. Thank goodness! This fantastic fighting game has a ton of Animal Crossing crossovers, including several stages based on the game – which change depending on your system's clock. Villager can attack opponents with his net, evade tough spots by flying away on a Gyroid, and plant a tree that packs a wallop when it falls. Isabelle remains her adorable self, even as she snags items with a fishing pole and bonks her rivals with street signs. If you haven't played a Smash Bros. game before, perhaps the Animal Crossing content is enough to lure you into one of the best series around.

This Stings!

Shake enough trees, and you're bound to get stung. Getting surprised by a wasp's nest is a part of life in Animal Crossing, and sometimes you're not fast enough with your net. Getting stung isn't fun, but there aren't any long-lasting effects. You can fix your status by purchasing or crafting medicine with the nest. If you get stung twice in one day, you'll faint and come to by your house. If you're on an island expedition, you'll awaken near the plane. It may be inconvenient, but don't worry – aside from a swollen eye, there aren't any real consequences.

Seasonality

Jan.	Feb.	Mar.	Apr.
May	June	*July*	*Aug.*
Sept.	Oct.	Nov.	Dec.

Current Active Hours

```
AM              PM
12      6       12      6
```

Common Butterfly

Fish

  L R

Sea bass

 Jump Display List Close Details

Checklists

Close

☑ Fish

☑ Insects

☑ Fossils

There are lots and lots of different fish, fossils, and bugs to collect in New Horizons – so many, in fact, that it's easy to lose track of all of them. Your Nook Phone's Critterpedia is a great in-game resource for info about the specimens that you've already found, but how do you get them all in the first place? Say you want to catch an oarfish. What time should you cast a line? Or how about a great white shark? Or a sea bass? OK, maybe you don't have to worry about that last one so much. Sorry.

Here's a rundown of every fish, fossil, and bug that you can collect in the game, where you can find them, and when. We've also allotted a little space for you to check off when you find these critters for the first time and if you've donated one to Blathers. Better yet, we've got the listed price for each one, so you can easily tell which items are worth the inventory space, and which ones can safely be discarded when inventory space is tight. Happy hunting!

Fish

Name	Location	Months Available	Time of Day	Value	Caught	Donated
Anchovy	Sea	All	4 AM-9 PM	200	☐	☐
Angelfish	River	May-October	4 PM-9 AM	3,000	☐	☐
Arapaima	River	June-September	4 PM-9 AM	10,000	☐	☐
Arowana	River	June-September	4 PM-9 AM	10,000	☐	☐
Barred Knifejaw	Sea	March-November	All	5,000	☐	☐
Barreleye	Sea	All	9 PM-4 AM	15,000	☐	☐
Betta	River	May-October	9 AM-4 PM	2,500	☐	☐
Bitterling	River	November-March	All	900	☐	☐
Black Bass	River	All	All	400	☐	☐
Blowfish	Sea	November-February	9 PM-4 AM	5,000	☐	☐
Blue Marlin	Pier	January-April, July-September, November-December	All	10,000	☐	☐
Bluegill	River	All	9 AM-4 PM	180	☐	☐
Butterfly Fish	Sea	April-September	All	1,000	☐	☐
Carp	Pond	All	All	300	☐	☐
Catfish	Pond	May-October	4 PM-9 AM	800	☐	☐
Char	Clifftop River / Pond	March-June, September-November	4 PM-9 AM	3,800	☐	☐
Cherry Salmon	Clifftop River	March-May, September-December	4 PM-9 AM	1,000	☐	☐
Clownfish	Sea	April-September	All	650	☐	☐
Coelacanth	Sea (While Raining)	All	All	15,000	☐	☐
Crawfish	Pond	April-September	All	200	☐	☐
Crucian Carp	River	All	All	160	☐	☐
Dab	Sea	October-April	All	300	☐	☐

Name	Location	Months Available	Time of Day	Value	Caught	Donated
Dace	River	All	4 PM-9 AM	240	☐	☐
Dorado	River	June-September	4 AM-9 PM	15,000	☐	☐
Football Fish	Sea	November-March	4 PM-9 AM	2,500	☐	☐
Freshwater Goby	River	All	4 PM-9 AM	400	☐	☐
Frog	Pond	May-August	All	120	☐	☐
Gar	Pond	June-September	4 PM-9 AM	6,000	☐	☐
Giant Snakehead	Pond	June-August	9 AM-4 PM	5,500	☐	☐
Giant Trevally	Pier	May-October	All	4,500	☐	☐
Golden Trout	Clifftop River	March-May, September-November	4 PM-9 AM	15,000	☐	☐
Goldfish	Pond	All	All	1,300	☐	☐
Great White Shark	Sea	June-September	4 PM-9 AM	15,000	☐	☐
Guppy	River	April-November	9 AM-4 PM	1,300	☐	☐
Hammerhead Shark	Sea	June-September	4 PM-9 AM	8,000	☐	☐
Horse Mackerel	Sea	All	All	150	☐	☐
Killifish	Pond	April-August	All	300	☐	☐
King Salmon	River Mouth	September	All	1,800	☐	☐
Koi	Pond	All	4 PM-9 AM	4,000	☐	☐
Loach	River	March-May	All	400	☐	☐
Mahi-Mahi	Pier	May-October	All	6,000	☐	☐
Mitten Crab	River	September-November	4 PM-9 AM	2,000	☐	☐
Moray Eel	Sea	August-October	All	2,000	☐	☐
Napoleonfish	Sea	July-August	4 AM-9 PM	10,000	☐	☐
Neon Tetra	River	April-November	9 AM-4 PM	500	☐	☐
Nibble Fish	River	May-September	9 AM-4 PM	1,500	☐	☐
Oarfish	Sea	December-May	All	9,000	☐	☐
Ocean Sunfish	Sea	July-September	4 AM-9 PM	4,000	☐	☐
Olive Flounder	Sea	All	All	800	☐	☐
Pale Chub	River	All	9 AM-4 PM	200	☐	☐
Pike	River	September-December	All	1,800	☐	☐
Piranha	River	June-September	9 AM-4 PM, 9 PM-4 AM	2,500	☐	☐

Name	Location	Months Available	Time of Day	Value	Caught	Donated
Pond Smelt	River	December-February	All	500	☐	☐
Pop-Eyed Goldfish	Pond	All	9 AM-4 PM	1,300	☐	☐
Puffer Fish	Sea	July-September	All	250	☐	☐
Rainbowfish	River	May-October	9 AM-4 PM	800	☐	☐
Ranchu Goldfish	Pond	All	9 AM-4 PM	4,500	☐	☐
Ray	Sea	August-November	4 AM-9 PM	3,000	☐	☐
Red Snapper	Sea	All	All	3,000	☐	☐
Ribbon Eel	Sea	June-November	All	600	☐	☐
Saddled Bichir	River	June-September	9 PM-4 AM	4,000	☐	☐
Salmon	River Mouth	September	All	700	☐	☐
Saw Shark	Sea	June-September	4 PM-9 AM	12,000	☐	☐
Sea Bass	Sea	All	All	400	☐	☐
Sea Butterfly	Sea	December-March	All	1,000	☐	☐
Sea Horse	River	April-November	All	1,100	☐	☐
Snapping Turtle	River	April-September	9 PM-4 AM	5,000	☐	☐
Soft-Shelled Turtle	Sea	August-September	4 PM-9 AM	3,750	☐	☐
Squid	Clifftop River	December-August	All	500	☐	☐
Stringfish	River Mouth	December-March	4 PM-9 AM	15,000	☐	☐
Sturgeon	River Mouth	September-March	All	10,000	☐	☐
Suckerfish	Sea	June-September	All	1,500	☐	☐
Surgeonfish	Sea	April-September	All	1,000	☐	☐
Sweetfish	River	July-September	All	900	☐	☐
Tadpole	Pond	March-July	All	100	☐	☐
Tilapia	River	June-October	All	800	☐	☐
Tuna	Pier	November-April	All	7,000	☐	☐
Whale Shark	Sea	October-March	All	13,000	☐	☐
Yellow Perch	River	October-March	All	300	☐	☐
Zebra Turkeyfish	Sea	April-November	All	500	☐	☐

Insects

Name	Location	Months Available	Time of Day	Value	Collected	Donated
Agrias Butterfly	Flying	April-September	8 AM-5 PM	3,000	☐	☐
Ant	On Spoiled Food	All	All	80	☐	☐
Atlas Moth	On Trees	April-September	7 PM-4 AM	3,000	☐	☐
Bagworm	Shaking Trees	All	All	600	☐	☐
Banded Dragonfly	Flying	May-October	8 AM-5 PM	4,500	☐	☐
Bell Cricket	On Ground	September-October	5 PM-8 AM	4430	☐	☐
Blue Weevil Beetle	On Trees	July-August	All	800	☐	☐
Brown Cicada	On Trees	July-August	8 AM-5 PM	250	☐	☐
Centipede	Under Rocks	September-June	4 PM-11 PM	300	☐	☐
Cicada Shell	On Trees	July-August	All	10	☐	☐
Citris Long-Horned Beetle	On Tree Stumps	All	All	350	☐	☐
Common Bluebottle	Flying	April-August	4 AM-7 PM	300	☐	☐
Common Butterfly	Flying	September-June	4 AM-7 PM	160	☐	☐
Cricket	On Ground	September-November	5 PM-8 AM	130	☐	☐
Cyclommatus Stag	On Coconut Trees	July-August	5 PM-8 AM	8,000	☐	☐
Damselfly	Flying	November-February	All	500	☐	☐
Darner Dragonfly	Flying	April-October	8 AM-5 PM	230	☐	☐
Diving Beetle	On Ponds and Rivers	May-September	8 AM-5 PM	800	☐	☐
Drone Beetle	On Trees	June-August	All	200	☐	☐
Dung Beetle	On Ground	December-February	All	3,000	☐	☐
Earth-Boring Dung Beetle	On Ground	July-September	All	300	☐	☐
Emperor Butterfly	Flying	December-March, June-September	5 PM-8 AM	4,000	☐	☐

Name	Location	Months Available	Time of Day	Value	Collected	Donated
Evening Cicada	On Trees	July-August	4 AM-8 AM, 4 PM-7 PM	550	☐	☐
Firefly	Flying	June	7 PM-4 AM	300	☐	☐
Flea	On Villagers	April-November	All	70	☐	☐
Fly	On Trash	All	All	60	☐	☐
Giant Cicada	On Trees	July-August	8 AM-5 PM	500	☐	☐
Giant Stag	On Trees	July-August	11 PM-8 AM	10,000	☐	☐
Giant Water Bug	On Ponds and Rivers	April-September	7 PM-4 AM	2,000	☐	☐
Giraffe Stag	On Trees	July-August	5 PM-8 AM	12,000	☐	☐
Golden Stag	On Coconut Trees	July-August	5 PM-8 AM	12,000	☐	☐
Goliath Beetle	On Coconut Trees	June-September	5 PM-8 AM	8,000	☐	☐
Grasshopper	On Ground	July-September	8 AM-5 PM	160	☐	☐
Great Purple Emperor	Flying	May-August	4 AM-7 PM	3,000	☐	☐
Hermit Crab	On the Beach	All	7 PM-8 AM	1,000	☐	☐
Honeybee	Flying	March-July	8 AM-5 PM	200	☐	☐
Horned Atlas	On Coconut Trees	June-July	5 PM-8 AM	8,000	☐	☐
Horned Dynastid	On Trees	June-July	5 PM-8 AM	1,350	☐	☐
Horned Elephant	On Coconut Trees	June-July	5 PM-8 AM	8,000	☐	☐
Horned Hercules	On Coconut Trees	June-July	5 PM-8 AM	12,000	☐	☐
Jewel Beetle	On Tree Stumps	April-August	All	2,400	☐	☐
Ladybug	On Flowers	March-June, September	8 AM-5 PM	200	☐	☐
Long Locust	On Ground	April-November	8 AM-5 PM	200	☐	☐
Madagascan Sunset Moth	Flying	April-September	8 AM-5 PM	2,500	☐	☐
Man-Faced Stink Bug	On Flowers	March-October	7 PM-8 AM	1,000	☐	☐
Mantis	On Flowers	March-November	8 AM-5 PM	430	☐	☐

Name	Location	Months Available	Time of Day	Value	Collected	Donated
Migratory Locust	On Ground	August-November	8 AM-5 PM	600	☐	☐
Miyama Stag	On Trees	July-August	All	1,000	☐	☐
Mole Cricket	Underground (Listen For Chirp)	November-May	All	500	☐	☐
Monarch Butterfly	Flying	September-November	4 AM-5 PM	140	☐	☐
Mosquito	Flying	June-August	5 PM-4 AM	130	☐	☐
Moth	Flying By Lights	All	7 PM-4 AM	130	☐	☐
Orchid Mantis	On White Flowers	March-November	8 AM-5 PM	2,400	☐	☐
Paper Kite Butterfly	Flying	All	8 AM-7 PM	1,000	☐	☐
Peacock Butterfly	Flying By Hybrid Flowers	March-June	4 AM-7 PM	2,500	☐	☐
Pill Bug	Under Rocks	September-June	11 PM-4 PM	250	☐	☐
Pondskater	On Ponds and Rivers	May-September	8 AM-7 PM	130	☐	☐
Queen Alexandra's Birdwing	Flying	May-September	8 AM-4 PM	4,000	☐	☐
Rainbow Stag	On Trees	June-September	7 PM-8 AM	6,000	☐	☐
Rajah Brooke's Birdwing	Flying	December-February, April-September	8 AM-5 PM	2,500	☐	☐
Red Dragonfly	Flying	August-September	8 AM-7 PM	180	☐	☐
Rice Grasshopper	On Ground	August-November	8 AM-7 PM	160	☐	☐
Robust Cicada	On Trees	July-August	8 AM-5 PM	300	☐	☐
Rosalia Batesi Beetle	On Tree Stumps	May-September	All	3,000	☐	☐
Saw Stag	On Trees	July-August	All	2,000	☐	☐
Scarab Beetle	On Trees	July-August	11 PM-8 AM	10,000	☐	☐
Scorpion	On Ground	May-October	7 PM-4 AM	8,000	☐	☐
Snail	On Rocks and Bushes During Rain	All	All	250	☐	☐

Name	Location	Months Available	Time of Day	Value	Collected	Donated
Spider	Shaking Trees	All	7 PM-8 AM	600	☐	☐
Stinkbug	On Flowers	March-October	All	120	☐	☐
Tarantula	On Ground	November-April	7 PM-4 AM	8,000	☐	☐
Tiger Beetle	On Ground	February-October	All	1,500	☐	☐
Tiger Butterfly	Flying	March-September	4 AM-7 PM	240	☐	☐
Violin Beetle	On Tree Stumps	May-June, September-November	All	450	☐	☐
Walker Cicada	On Trees	August-September	8 AM-5 PM	400	☐	☐
Walking Leaf	Under Trees	July-September	All	600	☐	☐
Walking Stick	On Trees	July-November	4 AM-8 AM, 5 PM-7 PM	600	☐	☐
Wasp	Shaking Trees	All	All	2,500	☐	☐
Wharf Roach	On Ocean Rocks	All	All	200	☐	☐
Yellow Butterfly	Flying	March-June, September-October	4 AM-7 PM	160		

I caught a mole cricket!
I really dug it!

Fossils

Name	Value	Collected	Donated
Acanthostega	2,000	☐	☐
Amber	1,200	☐	☐
Ammonite	1,100	☐	☐
Anklylo Skull	3,500	☐	☐
Ankylo Tail	2,500	☐	☐
Ankylo Torso	3,000	☐	☐
Anomalocaris	2,000	☐	☐
Archaopteryx	1,300	☐	☐
Archelon Skull	4,000	☐	☐
Archelon Tail	3,500	☐	☐
Australopith	1,100	☐	☐
Brachio Chest	5,500	☐	☐
Brachio Pelvis	5,000	☐	☐
Brachio Skull	6,000	☐	☐
Brachio Tail	5,500	☐	☐
Coprolite	1,100	☐	☐
Deinony Tail	2,500	☐	☐
Deinony Torso	3,000	☐	☐
Dimetrodon Skull	5,500	☐	☐
Dimetrodon Torso	5,000	☐	☐
Dinosaur Track	1,000	☐	☐
Diplo Chest	4,000	☐	☐
Diplo Neck	4,500	☐	☐
Diplo Pelvis	4,500	☐	☐
Diplo Skull	5,000	☐	☐
Diplo Tail	5,000	☐	☐
Diplo Tail Tip	4,000	☐	☐
Dunkleosteus	3,500	☐	☐
Eusthenopteron	2,000	☐	☐
Iguanodon Skull	4,000	☐	☐
Iguanodon Tail	3,000	☐	☐
Iguanodon Torso	3,500	☐	☐
Juramaia	1,000	☐	☐
Mammoth Skull	3,000	☐	☐
Mammoth Torso	2,500	☐	☐

Name	Value	Collected	Donated
Megacero Skull	4,500	☐	☐
Megacero Tail	3,000	☐	☐
Megacero Torso	3,500	☐	☐
Megalo Left Side	4,000	☐	☐
Megalo Right Side	5,500	☐	☐
Myllokunmingia	1,500	☐	☐
Ophthalmo Skull	2,500	☐	☐
Ophthalmo Torso	2,000	☐	☐
Pachysaurus Skull	4,000	☐	☐
Pachysaurus Tail	3,500	☐	☐
Parasaur Skull	3,500	☐	☐
Parasaur Tail	2,500	☐	☐
Parasaur Torso	3,000	☐	☐
Plesio Body	4,500	☐	☐
Plesio Skull	4,000	☐	☐
Plesio Tail	4,500	☐	☐
Prtera Body	4,000	☐	☐
Ptera Left Wing	4,500	☐	☐
Ptera Right Wing	4,500	☐	☐
Quetzal Left Wing	5,000	☐	☐
Quetzal Right Wing	5,000	☐	☐
Quetzal Torso	4,500	☐	☐
Sabertooth Skull	2,500	☐	☐
Sabertooth Tail	2,000	☐	☐
Shark-Tooth Pattern	1,000	☐	☐
Spino Skull	4,000	☐	☐
Spino Tail	2,500	☐	☐
Spino Torso	5,000	☐	☐
Stego Skull	5,000	☐	☐
Stego Tail	4,000	☐	☐
Stego Torso	4,500	☐	☐
T. Rex Skull	6,000	☐	☐
T. Rex Tail	5,000	☐	☐
T. Rex Torso	5,500	☐	☐
Tricera Skull	5,500	☐	☐
Tricera Tail	4,500	☐	☐
Tricera Torso	5,000	☐	☐
Trilobyte	1,300	☐	☐

Bianca

If I'm going to be a crazy-famous pop star, I need to explore the world and, like, experience stuff...

Don't go!

I'll be rooting for you!

Happy Trails!

Let's face it: Not every villager is going to click with you. There's no way to force them to leave, but if you ignore them long enough they'll eventually decide to move away on their own. You'll know they're ready if you see them walking around with what looks like a cloud over their head. Talk to them, and you can either ask them to stay or encourage them to leave. Once villagers decide to leave, your friends can visit in multiplayer and invite that villager to move into their island, provided they have the free space. It's a win-win!

ALSO AVAILABLE

WHEREVER BOOKS ARE SOLD

and at **WWW.TRIUMPHBOOKS.COM**

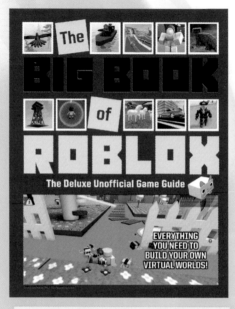